To Birdie,
Wishing you a happy stay in New Zealand,
With love from Uncle Norm and Cathie

Wishing you a happy stay in New Zealand,
With love from Uncle Norm and Cathie

New Zealand's SOUTH ISLAND in Colour

NEW ZEALAND'S
SOUTH ISLAND
IN COLOUR

PHOTOGRAPHS BY
KENNETH AND JEAN BIGWOOD

TEXT BY JIM HENDERSON

A. H. & A. W. REED
WELLINGTON · SYDNEY · LONDON

First published 1966
Reprinted 1970
Revised edition 1972
Reprinted 1973 (twice)
Reprinted 1976

A.H. & A.W. REED LTD

65-67 Taranaki Street, Wellington
53 Myoora Road, Terrey Hills, Sydney 2084
11 Southampton Row, London WC1B 5HA
also
16 Beresford Street, Auckland
165 Cashel Street, Christchurch

© 1966. 1972 A. H. & A. W. REED
ISBN 0 589 00275 9

Library of Congress Catalog Card Number: 72-75989

KYODO PRINTING COMPANY LTD, TOKYO, JAPAN

INTRODUCTION

HERE IS an artist's most beautiful proof that New Zealand does not end at Cook Strait....

But the South is not all mountain and lake, all jumble and splash. We are beginning to try to work out how our people fit into the landscape now, and what it *means* to us. We are settling into our own country. Home is here now, right here, like this:

Nelson, the province of blue and gold, so still, heavy with fruit, not a leaf stirring in the slavishly-nursed tobacco fields or pungent hop gardens; bronzed Marlborough (smelling of grease from the fleece, and proud of it) where the merino and Molesworth look down like symbols saying "Don't muck around; get on with the job"; powerful Canterbury, a brown youth striding the great plains and rivers, a kea flying ahead, and the Alps to stop folk falling over the edge; Otago of goldrush and apricots, of brains and human care, and an inland atmosphere felt nowhere else in New Zealand; Southland of the laconic roving fishing fleet, the sweeping green plains like another harvesting sea, then the mighty climax of her fiords; Westland, greenstone Eldorado of the Maori, where, praise be, materialism counts for little and the braggart wins only a smile, where the rain can't dampen or rust or blackberry smother the warmest and most humorous hearts in New Zealand.

But it has taken over a hundred years' sweat to hack and hew and hammer some shape and sense (from the civilised viewpoint) into this country. The poet or writer mooning about with pencil and paper was (and sometimes still is) a most irritating sight to the primitive toiler; we have been flooded with writings, songs, and readymade folklore in turn from Britain, then the United States, and finally from Australia. Our family life has been raked alternately by savage depressions and wars — an average of 1,000 war casualties each year for a century. A baby in battledress.

May Maori blood, zest, and sense of kinship add more happiness, eloquence, and song to the brew in the years to come.

For 75 years New Zealand was a group of islands somehow superimposed above Britain. Then the butcheries of Europe moved us to around what was called the Middle East and "the lifeline of Empire". The Vietnam war had New Zealand unhappily and uneasily squatting in South-east Asia. With luck and moderate fallout within the next 20 years we'll be thinking and acting for ourselves for a change, in the South-west Pacific where we actually happen to be, a most important part of Polynesia, with its own particular contribution to evolve and to give to the world and to humanity.

JIM HENDERSON

DEDICATION

To those in hospital; to those who may journey no more in body; to those whose toil and hope are woven into the pattern; to those who smile and remember; to the better breed of tomorrow; to those of the North Island and of other lands who have not yet visited the South Island,

GREETINGS

New Zealand's NORTH ISLAND in Colour

Kenneth and Jean Bigwoods's companion volume is identical in format to this book, and with it completes an outstanding photographic coverage of New Zealand. The text for *New Zealand's NORTH ISLAND in Colour* is written by L. J. Wild.

THE PLATES

U NLESS he or she is bound for prison (or possibly for boarding school) the returning South Islander's heart gives an extra twinge and the blood runs faster when ship or plane presents once more the blue-and-green jigsaw of Marlborough Sounds, or the great sweeping sandy sickle of Cape Farewell.

The sun-mellow waterways of the Sounds stretch from Picton and Port Underwood to D'Urville Island—take your pick, there's room for all and more; city refugee and weekend car-polisher, boatman, fisherman, running overflowing children, elderly retired couples with pictures of easily-run cottages above that small scrub-scented bay, water skiers, picnickers, auctioneers and undertakers, campers and trampers.

This, like the whole of New Zealand in fact, could be part of a World Sanatorium if the nations were truly united. Asked about the Sounds he works, lives, and thinks in, Adrian Hayter, the world-circling lone sailor and Scott Base leader, wrote:

Surely in the Sounds we face the same danger faced by every beauty spot in the world, which, when made easily and comfortably available to the many, soon denies even to the few the very quality it originally provided. The main quality of the Marlborough Sounds is their spacious, natural, and unspoilt variety, and such areas of the country are to become increasingly important as havens in which we may recuperate and restore our sense of balance.

PLATE 1
View over the Tawhitinui Reach of Pelorus Sound, towards Mount Shewell, 2,770 feet, on the road to French Pass, Marlborough Sounds.

THIS FARM, owned by the Murray family for some 90 years, has been growing barley for most of that time—it does well, and it pays reasonably well. What's more, in 1912, barley grown here won first prize at the World Fair held in Panama. The fate of this crop in the picture, a particularly good one yielding 125 bushels to the acre, was to be sent to a stockfoods mill at Nelson to be processed for pig and poultry food.

A good thing about barley—quite apart from its cheerful malt-making properties—is that it can be grown for many years in the same ground without running down the fertility of the soil. To watch a properly ripened crop waving gently in a summer sunset is one of the rewards treasured by a good farmer.

The distinctive feature of Carlsberg barley, bred in Denmark and imported by the Crop Research Division of the DSIR, is the reddish eyles, ails, awns, or beards, which appear as the seedheads form and remain until the crop ripens off to a uniform golden hue rather like that of a well-baked sponge-cake.

In 1820 the Rev. John Butler reaped 12 bushels of barley; New Zealand now produces more than 4,000,000 bushels of barley a year, the malting, brewing, and distilling industry taking more than half of it. Most of New Zealand's barley grows in the area from North Canterbury down to North Otago.

PLATE 2
Heading Carlsberg barley, near Spring Creek, Blenheim, Marlborough.

AND JUST a few weeks ago, weren't these only tiny brown and black seeds, and a plan and an intention in a man's mind? The stream chuckling to the young, with the sun itself on holiday today, was once upon a time the water race and overflow for Parker's flour mill nearby, from about 1880 to 1905.

"Pollard Park's 58 acres of ground were laid out by the late James Oliver, a London-trained landscape and horticultural expert, after World War One," writes Norman Brayshaw, secretary of the Marlborough Historical Society. The large trees of today were planted as a memorial to Marlborough men killed in that war. At first, little money about hampered progress, but development work continues with grants from the Blenheim Borough Council.

Near the centre of the Park is the Centennial Rose Garden. This is the work of the Marlborough Rose Society, commemorating Marlborough's first centennial of separation from Nelson Province in 1859. What's more, the Society cares for and tends the thousand rose-trees of this garden.

And further small seeds must have been sown in the minds of two small boys in a distant little Marlborough primary school beside the sweeping Pelorus Sound at Havelock, the old and early school of Lord Rutherford of Nelson, the blacksmith's son who cracked the atom on the anvil of his mind; and of Doctor William Pickering, a leading scientist among America's rocket and space experts.

PLATE 3
Colourful gardens at Pollard Park, Blenheim.

OUR WEALTH is balanced on a blade of grass.

Fields like these no more grew up by themselves than cities did. First the bush had to be felled and burnt—ordeal for Aotearoa by axe, saw and flame—and at the turn of the century immigrants coming to New Zealand could smell our bushfires from halfway across the Tasman Sea. A million million birdsongs vanished forever in the crackling smoke as the settlers slew 75 per cent of our native forests.

A battlefield of sprawling, blackened stumps, logs, dead trees (each, like stricken soldiers, in its own special position), had to be cleared out of the way, laboriously, piece by piece over the years. And the fences too (and O! the fencers' thirst on a dry, remote rocky ridge!), which would stretch from here to the moon five times—1,000,000 to 1,200,000 miles of fences, say.

When tussocks, not forests, covered future farmlands they were burnt off, a practice now frowned on because it denudes the hillsides and causes erosion.

The few native grasses, except maybe Danthonia, proved poor stuff for the avalanches of eroding animals coming into the country. English grasses came to the rescue, and with them too came the weeds, as well as (a naturalist notes) "the dear well-remembered wild flowers and fruits of the distant Homeland—sweet briar, periwinkle, and blackberry".

Here is the old-time bushburn recipe for fortune: take 20 lb of certified perennial ryegrass, 5 to 8 lb of Italian ryegrass, 5 lb of cocksfoot, 2 lb of white clover, 1 lb of red clover, 2 lb of browntop and 2 lb of crested dogstail. Mix together, divide into handy bags, and handful by handful, tramp backwards and forwards through the blackened logs, sowing the seed from North Cape to Bluff, with small local variations and preferences according to climates and soils.

Then, call in Science and aircraft and brains for the problems to come.

PLATE 4
Sheep, sunlight, shadows, Kaituna Valley, Blenheim-Nelson highway.

IN MARLBOROUGH you will see merinos in groups standing under matagouri trees, heads down, escaping the heat of the day. They look alike—gnarled grey sheep and thorny grey matagouri, both tough and enduring—the matagouri to the point of defiance—symbolic of the windy gorges and the high tops where the longhaired tussock sweeps and sways. And in the dusty riverbeds, living on apparently nothing, both sheep and plant are still healthy and strong. But the matagouri knew the moa.

In Marlborough well-bred stud merino rams will shear from 20 to 28 lb of wool, and in some cases as high as 30lb. Ewes shear up to 18 lb.

Tapuaenuku, the snowy sentinel of Cook Strait clearly seen from Wellington, is taller than any North Island mountain. It was first climbed in 1864 by a 25-year-old local farmer, Nehemiah McRae of Blairich Station in the valley, who had come to New Zealand in 1842 as the two-year-old son of a pioneering Scottish family. Like so many early settlers or their children, Nehemiah met "the New Zealand death": drowned when crossing the flooded Awatere River on horseback. His last words were: "Farewell; remember me."

Young Edmund Hillary, when a member of the Air Force stationed at Woodbourne, climbed Tapuaenuku three times in winter, learning many valuable mountaineering lessons.

The name means "the footsteps of the rainbow god".

PLATE 5
Dumgree Station, Awatere Valley, Mount Tapuaenuku and matagouri

IN POURING RAIN, appropriately enough, a small gathering of historically minded Nelsonians watched an explorer's great-grandson, James T. Lewis of Richmond, unveil and dedicate a bronze plaque here on a wet November day in 1961, to commemorate the Nelson Provincial Government surveyors, dogged and durable men, whose discoveries and notebooks opened the ways for our roads and our future.

Henry Lewis, son of an Essex surveyor, auctioneer and landowner, with his wife Susannah, migrated with their eight children, first to Canada (too cold), then to Melbourne (too hot), and so to New Zealand. Christopher Maling had been born in Nelson a few months after the death at the Wairau affray of his father, Thomas Maling, Chief Constable at Nelson. Together, the two discovered the Lewis Pass, March-April 1860, although the Maoris, using the Pass over many years to get precious greenstone for ornaments and weapons, had it all but signposted.

Maling, back there a year later, wrote: "We were detained here for two days by heavy rain, which made the river too high for us to cross; but as the river fell on the third day, we started down the Boyle, crossing or rather wading down it nearly the whole way ($5\frac{1}{2}$ miles), on account of the thick growth of wild-irishmen, spaniard, and speargrass, which grew on either bank, entirely preventing our making any progress."

PLATE 6
Beech forest and mountains on the Lewis Pass highway linking the east and west coasts of the South Island.

"A LOVELY VILLAGE, Kaikoura, nestles as a village should, between steep limestone cliffs and the sea," writes a local squatter. "Behind tower the splendid mountains, snow-covered for most of the year; in front the glorious sweep of the bay, stretching as far as the eye can see, until the sea and mountains appear to melt together in the far-off haze."

Up in the whipped-cream mountains lies New Zealand's largest station, Molesworth, stretching from 3,000 to 6,000 feet above the sea-haze. To every farmer, farm-worker, and country dog worth his salt, the name "Molesworth" rings within, as the name of one particular battle echoes inevitably through an old soldier's lifetime.

There are presidents and premiers galore—but only one manager of Molesworth.

The largest run in New Zealand, 449,970 acres, today carries about 8,000 head of cattle and a mere 400 sheep. On just one part of today's Molesworth up to 50,000 sheep were once shorn, but disaster came through severe burning of hillsides, rabbits swarming in millions like lice ("whole hillsides moving with rabbits, their warrens like raisins in a cake"), then erosion and deer-and-goat plagues, plus several exceptionally severe winters killing sheep by the thousands.

The Department of Lands and Survey stepped in, removed the sheep, unfolded long-term plans, and opened full-scale warfare including aerial poisoning against the rabbit—over $400,000 has been spent to master the furry pest since the Crown took over in 1938. Aircraft, playing many parts,

joined in restoration work, sowing over 35,000 acres with cocksfoot and red clover, and Molesworth returned to life with cattle gradually coming back since 1941.

This conspicuous success, reviving ruined land in the mountains, has interested overseas ranchers, foresters, conservation officers and professional agriculturists.

But the old hands, like Bruce Stronach in his book *Musterer on Molesworth*, chant:

Land of rocks and rivers deep,
Lousy with dogs and merino sheep,
Squatter's paradise, musterer's hell—
Molesworth Station, fare you well!

PLATE 7
The Seaward Kaikoura mountains reflected in tidal waters, near Kaikoura township.

NEW ZEALAND developed a new world breed with the Corriedale sheep. The aim was to produce a sheep which would range almost as high and as wide in the mountains as the merino, but produce much better meat.

This revolutionary move began in North Otago, at Corriedale Station, where the owner, James Little, carried out his ideas from 1866–68. The breed was perfected, to become an international favourite. Exports began to other sheep-breeders overseas in the late 1880s, first in South America where more Corriedales graze today than any other breed, and in Australia where this sheep is now the next favourite after the merino.

The distinctive (and certainly adaptable) breed received a warm welcome as well in the frigid Falkland Islands, the United States, South Africa, Kenya, China, and Japan, and has been used for improving certain local breeds in Israel, Roumania, and Russia. Corriedales outnumber merinos by more than two to one in New Zealand today.

Before Corriedale stud ewes are sold to start a new flock, for the protection of the buyers a Corriedale Sheep Society inspector examines and tattooes them in one ear with a C inside a circle.

The Society has its own publication *The Corriedale* in Christchurch; has sent breeders abroad to keep in touch with sheep developments and needs in other climates and lands; has held several world conferences since the first in Christchurch in 1960; and appoints its own inspectors "whose approval must be given to any sheep, whether a registered pedigree animal or commercial grade, before it can be sold for export as a "New Zealand Corriedale".

PLATE 10
Bringing in a mob of Corriedale sheep for crutching, Mendip Hills Station, North Canterbury.

HUTT IS OVER 7,000 feet, a blocky, chunky, not particularly attractive mountain, yet "high mountains are a feeling". The gorge is a stark, grim, deep gulch pounded

THAT WIRY and wrinkled old bedouin of North Africa and Spain, the merino, came to New Zealand with the early settlers by way of Australia, where for some time it had been the only breed. But this kind of sheep was unsuitable for wet areas and rich flats. Other breeds pushed them out.

Eventually they found their permanent home in the dry areas and tussocky uplands, mainly in the South Island from Marlborough to Otago. Tallied up today, they would number just over a million.

As much as that wry comedian the kea, merinos have become a part of this kind of country with huge areas to roam. John Scott of Godley Peaks, which is one of the highest and most rugged of the Mackenzie Country runs, says he has found merino wethers at 7,500 feet. Well away from strange noises, nervous humans, and distracting cities, they settle down and grow beautiful wool as fine as silk—in fact billiard-table cloth is made from the finest merino wool.

"I saw some yesterday grazing in the Mackenzie Country, a plain of poor danthonia and scab weed," writes an ex-merino man, Gerald Goulter, touring south and obviously not referring to this specific farm. "The old merino, his gaunt frame fitting into the landscape of sharp hills and hard plains. He was sold at Tekapo sale for NZ$7.70, still the same old frame I have seen sold for a bob in bad years.

"They are a pleasure to muster, free-running and wild.

"With his beautiful wool, silky nose and clean habits, the merino is undoubtedly the aristocrat of the sheep world."

PLATE 16
Mustering merino sheep, Clent Hills Station Ashburton Gorge.

"I AM NOT SURE that Mount Cook is not the finest in outline of all the snowy mountains I have ever seen. No one can mistake it. If a person says he thinks he has seen Mount Cook, you may be quite sure that he has not seen it. The moment it comes into sight the exclamation is 'that is Mount Cook', not 'that must be Mount Cook'. There is no possibility of mistake. . . . Though it is hazardous to say this of any mountain, I do not think that any human being will ever reach its top." (Samuel Butler)

But on Christmas Day 1894 "we were gleefully shaking hands on the highest point of New Zealand"—three New Zealand-born young men had made it, and for the first time ever: George Graham, Waimate; Tom Fyfe, Timaru; and 19-year-old Jack Clarke, Temuka. Fyfe recorded: "I regretfully thought—there is but one Aorangi."

Many women have climbed the mountain: Mavis Davidson, Sheila MacMurray, and Doreen Pickens (now Urquhart) made up the first all-woman team on 6 January 1953.

A good trip for a young climber learning mountaincraft would be in a party from The Hermitage, across the Southern Alps to the Fox or Franz Josef Glacier and back again by Graham Saddle and Copland Pass. Next season, a straightforward 10,000-foot peak, and then, as experience accumulates, he or she can think about Mount Cook. On Mount Cook a first-class guide would take with him no more than two experienced climbers. They'd be roped together most of the time with a light nylon rope, to check a fall or a sudden slide down hidden crevasses. Most of the big climbs start and end in the dark, climbers using headlamps rather like a miner's light.

Harry Ayres, one of Mount Cook's most experienced guides, had climbed that mountain 14 times before he was 40. "Sometimes the top of Mount Cook is so calm you can strike a match, and the flame is perfectly steady until the match burns right away," says Harry. "And even up there on the top of Mount Cook you'll still find the perpetual blowfly."

PLATE 18
Mount Cook and alpine flowers in the Hooker Valley.

"THE CLIMBER knows the pure joy of hand on rock and boot on ice; the pre-dawn start, the morning star and the looming bulk of the mountain, *his mountain for a day*.

"The lonely call of a kea in the darkness and, as the light comes in and rolls back the mist, the desolation of the valley far below.

"Then the sun and the colour and glow and awareness of height and danger and steady crunch of crampons. Crash and roar and speed of an avalanche, filling the valley with thunder then blotting it out with a cloud of ice particles. . . ."

So write Reg and Roey Winn, husband and wife, of Christchurch, remembering climbing days. Remembering as climbers can, and do, the wide world over, and balancing a peak upon a pencil-point.

PLATE 19
Mount Sefton, 10,350 feet, and White Horse Hill, Mount Cook National Park.

THEY GO OUT in all weathers to keep the markets supplied.

Boats cruise and quest from Timaru south-about to the West Coast fiords, seeking all kinds of fish. Trawlers land soles, flounders, brill, small groper, elephant fish, rigs, ling; line-boats land mainly blue cod, groper, and ling. Cray boats concentrate on crayfish pots during their season, and line and trawl out of the cray season. The wet fish catch landed in Otago ports in a year is worth to the fishermen about NZ$393,000.00 and with crayfish and oysters included in the return NZ$3,610,700.00.

"Weather round the Otago and West Coast parts of the South Island can be rough and dangerous," one mariner said, "especially to cray boats fishing close into rocky shores. Mishaps are numerous and don't make the headlines; fishermen chalk these up as experience and laugh them off, something to tell their mates when they meet over a glass. Engines break down, a boat catches fire, a call for assistance goes out and is promptly answered by all boats in the vicinity, regardless of cost. That is the law of the sea."

On an average, he thought, two boats may be lost each year.

PLATE 20
Fishing fleet riding at anchor on a boisterous day, Moeraki Bay, Otago

DID SOME SPACECRAFT from the galaxy of Appapathachet land here, and eventually turn to stone, awaiting further orders from staff officers at Base?

No, say old stories: a doomed Maori canoe, Araiteuru, stormdriven helplessly through the mists of legends, vanished in the spray of centuries, but its gourds and baskets washed ashore, to remain, to remind, to glint under the moon and the midnight frost.

More prosaically: "These boulders are the most perfect examples of their kind that have been found anywhere in either the northern or southern hemispheres. They consist mainly of carbonate of lime, silica, alumina, and peroxide of iron," writes G.B. Stevenson in *Maori and Pakeha in North Otago.* "They are formed around a central core of carbonate of lime crystals, which appears to have the power of attracting and consolidating the above ingredients from the adjacent soil which contains them in the right proportions. The shape is not due to the action of the sea."

PLATE 21
The strange, symmetrical Moeraki boulders on the coast south of Oamaru, Otago

DUNEDIN (the ancient name of Scotland's Edinburgh), was founded in 1848. It was to be the focal point of the settlement of Otago, intended by the founders to be a Scottish Presbyterian settlement, but its original character was dramatically altered by the shiploads of prospectors who arrived in thousands after the discovery of gold in Otago by Gabriel Read at Tuapeka (commonly known as Gabriel's Gully) in 1861.

Within two years the population of Otago Province leapt from 12,600 to over 60,000, and Dunedin became for a while the largest town in New Zealand. As many as 2,000 a day passed through Dunedin, notes the historian Keith Sinclair, and the sober inhabitants were horrified at the sudden appearance of saloons, gambling dens, billiard rooms, and dancehalls to attract the new gold.

But, unlike the dozens of mushroom gold towns that appeared in the bush overnight to provide these blowsy amenities and then disappeared again when the gold and its miners had gone, Dunedin was able to absorb some of the new wealth in money and immigrants to its permanent benefit, and it remained our leading commercial centre until 1900.

Until this time too the South Island held the balance of political power as the increased population gave Southerners control of the General Assembly. Gold provided the finance for many of the fine public works in Dunedin, including the University of Otago (New Zealand's oldest university), which today is particularly famous for its medical, dental, and theological schools.

PLATE 22
The city of Dunedin, from Signal Hill, looking south.

"ON 3 MAY 1820, by the plough for the first time was New Zealand soil upturned....we can let it go at that", records our great naturalist, H. Guthrie-Smith, in his *Sorrows and Joys of a New Zealand Naturalist*. "Nothing could more clearly indicate the deplorable spirit of these times than that a good man could write thus of an operation destined to dislodge wholesale the bittern (*Ardea poeciloptila*), the pukeko (*Porphyrio melanonotus*) the fernbird (*Sphenoeacus punctatus*), and several species of small rail." But "I trust", wrote the Rev. J.G. Butler, himself the apostolic puncher of his bullock team, "that this auspicious day will be remembered with gratitude and its anniversary kept by ages yet unborn."

The size and the richness of the rolling Southland plains astonish the visitor. Invercargill, a city of integrity, sets an example to the rest of New Zealand by running its own hotels and liquor trade with conspicuous success; and at Bluff and Stewart Island (whose distinctive quiet beauty, trusting woodhens, and calm twilights haunt and echo years later) integration between Pakeha and Maori already has taken place, and nobody makes a fuss about it.

Southland is proud of its blood links with Scotland but, with good Presbyterian reserve, not unreasonably so. Radio Invercargill had a weekly programme called "A Sprig of Heather". "But," said the grand-daughter of a grand old Southlander who could speak Gaelic and knew Robert Burns backwards, "Grandfather never listens to 'A Sprig of Heather' *unless there are visitors*."

PLATE 23
Spring ploughing on farmlands in Croydon Bush district, near Gore, Southland.

"WESTERN SHORE formed by the snowy Alps with grand lofty peaks and pinnacles, domes and cones, rents and clefts of all sizes and form." After a tough slog overland, C. J. Nairn wrote this in his diary on 27 January 1852. On that day he and his companion W. Stephen were the first Europeans to see Lake Te Anau.

Today, thousands of tourists pass by this lake on the way to Hollyford and Milford, while Te Anau town itself each year sees more holiday-makers, hunters, anglers, and boat-owners. Nearly 3,000 visitors a season hike along a world-famous three-day walk, the Milford Track, which begins at the head of the lake.

Te Anau (the name of a chieftainess: the lake of many arms; the rain on the water—to give but three of many versions), stretching over 38 miles and from 1 to 6 miles across, is our second largest lake in New Zealand, next after Taupo.

Among Nairn's "grand lofty peaks" of the lake's western shore, Dr G. B. Orbell, with 50 yards of fishing net and a camera, rediscovered and photographed the "extinct" flightless notornis or takahe in November 1948.

This is the Land of the Lost Tribe, legends say.

"From time to time," writes a Southland historian, F. W. G. Miller in *West to the Fiords*, "there have been stories of mysterious sounds heard by deerstalkers only a few feet away in the bush, of a sudden chattering of voices that have died away to nothing as the startled listeners have risen to their feet to peer vainly through the wall of leaves. Some explorers have even claimed to have seen fresh naked footprints where no white man could possibly have trodden."

PLATE 24
The South Fiord of Lake Te Anau, from the Dome Islands, looking towards snow-capped Mount Maury.

HERE AND THERE throughout New Zealand men dream about an immense strip of Western Southland called Fiordland National Park—3,300,000 acres of it, large parts of it still unexplored.

These men live out 49 weeks of the year so that for the remaining three weeks they can clear out, to Lake Te Anau, to land by launch or amphibian aircraft on some secret beach like this; and then, laden like a Friday-night housewife, strike inland and up through dark rainforest to the blonde tussock and snowgrass of the tops, to Wapiti Country, the only spot in the Southern Hemisphere where wapiti roam at liberty. (And where, perhaps, to the west, there may still be a shy, flitting herd of Saskatchewan moose, remnants of an acclimatisation experiment that failed.)

Some 60 deerstalkers, selected by ballot, go in for a strictly limited season to shoot the big creamy-brown wapiti (known in America as elk), 18 of which were first let loose here in 1905.

And round some distant camp fire tonight, someone could be recalling the name of some veteran wapiti shooter such as McKenzie of Leithen Downs, Herrick from Havelock North, Donald of Masterton, McConochie of Nelson, Morris of Woodville. . . .

"You can bring it back and see it in your mind anytime," explained one enthusiast, Frank Tully. "Not just the killing, but the satisfaction and achievement. That tricky corner of the flooded river you had to cross; your carefully chosen plans and gear standing up to the wear and tear and strain; the properly pitched tent, dry as a chip inside with the rain hammering down; that great wapiti bull bugling away and beyond, and the immense mountains all around. You've been born again."

PLATE 25
Dock Bay, Lake Te Anau, a sweep of sandy shore beneath the beech trees.

AVALANCHES permitting, the road from Te Anau to Milford is comfortable enough today.

Spectacular to both impressionable tourist and thoughtful engineer, this road passes along two valleys of great beauty, the Eglinton and the Hollyford; climbs to 3,000 feet and vanishes into the Homer Tunnel, emerging three-quarters of a mile later from the solid rock to zigzag down a canyon to Milford: altogether 74 miles from Te Anau. About 60,000 people make this trip every year.

The old explorer Henry Homer died in forgotten poverty, with only five people at his funeral; but the tunnel, and the hopes he pleaded for in 1889, came true in the end, 50 years later, when most other hopes were dying.

For in the dark Depression of the 'thirties this road and tunnel began: first a 19-mile strip, made with shovels and wheelbarrows, from Te Anau to Te Anau Downs, in 1929. A year later, the planners decided to continue the road on, to open up the Eglinton flats. By 1934 (New Zealand's unemployed reached 68,500 then) the road had covered 49 miles, travelling through the beauty and isolation of the Eglinton Valley to the Divide, where the Hollyford Valley begins.

This is one view the unemployed of the 'thirties have given us today, from the Divide, 1,740 feet high, looking to Mount Lyttle.

PLATE 26
Mount Lyttle from the Divide, Eglinton Valley, on the highway to Milford Sound.

THE HOLLYFORD VALLEY: bush, rough river and, pressing close on either side, sheer mountains, the bush falling away like a climber growing dizzy and giving up to the bare rock brown and grey and black, and then, higher yet, the first covering of snow.

And so to the Homer Tunnel, with a great ring of mountains standing in close, 6,000 to 8,000 feet high. . . .

Cabinet in Wellington brought in another hundred unemployed men, the road would thrust on, to Milford. So in July 1935 five men, the first of a select and stubborn band, began the first excavation for the tunnel, using shovels and wheelbarrows. Heavy snows fell in the winter; the rain averaged 250 inches a year.

They bored away into that mountain of rock until they were sick of the sight of stones. A tourist from Newfoundland came and said in astonishment: "We live in a wonderful age."

"Yes," agreed Kelly the points-man, "the blessed Stone Age."

Three men on the job, L. P. Overton, D. F. Hulse, and T. W. Smith were killed in avalanches.

The hole pierced through in February 1940. Work stopped in 1942 because of the War, resumed in March 1951, and finished, the task complete, with the same contractor, in 1953.

People like Homer and the roadmen who came after him should have been given a campaign medal.

PLATE 27
Upper Hollyford River, looking upstream to Students Peak, Fiordland National Park.

IF YOU HAD the chance of making just one trip in your life in New Zealand, this is it—over to Milford Sound, guarded by Mitre Peak, a sentinel standing 5,560 feet high.

All around is immensity looking over your shoulder. *It is all so close:* waterfalls hundreds of feet high, rock forming gigantic castles and turrets, and all reflected in the great fiord far below.

In one place an immense wall rises 3,000 feet, straight up. Some classical story, or an opera, will eventually come from this rock-and-water land which you've only imagined before from *Grimm's Fairy Tales*.

You weary from looking up in astonishment; you weary from wondering; you weary from being a beetle. Yet Milford gives, too, a clean, uplifted feeling.

You come away feeling very small, little more than some meagre dry brown leaf, because (as a businessman told me), "It puts you in your proper perspective."

What if the Parliament Buildings had been built here, instead of a luxury hotel?

PLATE 28
High snow on Mitre Peak and low tide in Milford Sound.

A SIGHT to warm the heart of any New Zealander— the rough hustling mountain stream, the brown pools and broad boulders (watch your step), the sopping moss with whiskery little towers, and ferns and the crouching, crowding bush.

Perhaps a whistling duck—or a tiny crayfish, on guard? "You have a rest, I can't. You have a rest, I can't," an old South Island goldminer believed the busy streams were always telling him. . . .

Through the Homer Tunnel, down the Cleddau Canyon by the rainbow mists of waterfalls, to the head of Milford Sound—the climax of the journey. On the way, past The Chasm, where this river's angry water has slashed a great battleaxe gash in the rock, in the shadows and the foam, two giant dark faces watch each other—stone faces—Maori faces?

In most winters the road twisting through Hollyford and Cleddau is swept with at least one avalanche to the mile, so the highway is closed from June to early October. But sightseeing aircraft continue their breathtaking flights into Fiordland, amazing and delighting New Zealand and overseas tourists alike.

Why Cleddau? It's named after the River Cleddau, which also flows into a Milford Haven, but on the other side of the world, in Pembrokeshire, Wales. The Maori name for Milford is Piopiotahi, meaning a pioneering Maori canoe; or else a solitary native thrush, which came here not as a tourist but sorrowing and in grief, after the death of the adventurous god Maui.

PLATE 29
Upper Cleddau River on the highway to Milford Sound.

THE GOLDMINERS were playing up in Heaven, behaving too boisterously, reminiscing much too vigorously, carrying out far too many alarming practical jokes. At length, after a particularly violent explosion (says an old Central Otago story) St Peter, distressed, visited in secret a prominent miner, and begged him to do something about it all.

"Perhaps....perhaps a rumour that they've struck it rich in Hell?" suggested the saint.

The word got around, and in no time the goldrush was on, with jubilant miners, packs up and gear clanking, streaming over the clouds, away from Heaven, bound for elsewhere.

Among the migrants, St Peter saw to his astonishment the conspirator miner who had spread the rumour so successfully.

"Why—surely not—why are you going too?" asked the puzzled saint.

"You never can tell," called back the goldminer in farewell. "There might be some truth in it after all."

However, returning to Earth again, scattered here and there over parts of Central Otago, by riverflat or gorge, lie the remains of the dry stone walls and the grey stone cottages the miners built. Handy caves, too, made homes.

If the gold or the work lasted long enough, some raised families—a childhood which could never be forgotten.

Among the stacked stones and debris they left behind them, you will still see a flowering rosebush or a clump of spring daffodils.

PLATE 30
Old mining days cottage at Arrowtown, Central Otago.

IN CONVERSATION, a shepherd around these pleasant parts suddenly looked glum, shook his head, grey with the years, and remarked pensively: "Ah yes. But just wait till the boom gets to us."

"What's the matter? Prices for wool and meat aren't so bad now, and. . . . ."

"No, no!" said the old man impatiently. "I mean the *atomic* boom."

But few countryside folk are true pessimists at heart, and much thought goes into planning ahead, and preparing for future flocks and crops.

An important aspect of this is growing seed, which is examined and approved for purity and germination (or "certified" as they say) by the Department of Agriculture before being sold at home or to some 30 countries abroad. Each year, South Island farmers set aside about at least 160,000 acres—sometimes considerably more—for growing the seeds of grasses, clover, and lucerne. Canterbury accounts for about 70 per cent, with Otago, Southland and Marlborough filling the rest.

Ryegrasses are grown the most, New Zealand producing on the way to 2 million bushels. Up to nearly 6 million lbs of white clover seed can be raised a year, usually followed in quantity by crested dogstail, cocksfoot, and the red clovers.

Large amounts of grass and clover seed have been exported in recent years to give a tidy export income of about NZ$4 million. The main customers are, in order of importance, Australia, the United Kingdom, and France.

PLATE 31
Sideraking hay, Gibbston, Kawarau Valley. Nevis bluff in background.

A MONSTER lives at the bottom of Wakatipu, this "lake that breathes", the old Maoris said, and as proof, why, see for yourself: the curious regular rising and falling of the level of the lake—that's the monster breathing away down below. As it happens, the lake, 1,239 feet deep, goes down to more than 200 feet below sea level.

Wise men, glasses glinting, explain that glaciers carved many of our South Island lakes, but others look into the fireside embers of night and tell how the great lakes were dug with the heroic wooden spade of that typhoon of a Maori chief and explorer, Te Raikaihaitu, the man who beat the bulldozer.

Of all the memories and attractions of Wakatipu's playtown Queenstown—from skiing grounds on nearby Coronet Peak, to the old gold-dust trails, to scenic air flights over a southern mesh of lake and mountain—one memory may remain curiously apart: within the town's generous park, spilling with colour from flowerbeds and shrubs, a great boulder lies, left behind by a long-ago glacier, and now inscribed in homage to Scott of the Antarctic.

PLATE 33
The home paddocks of Closeburn Station, Lake Wakatipu, on the Queenstown/Glenorchy road.

HERE IS A VISION, captured and preserved, which thousands of New Zealand prisoners of war longed for, and drew hope and strength from, in the dull, dead, trampled earth and foot-shuffling life of barbed wire cages. Memories like this saved lives and reinforced that determination to return.

And this, too, is the vision which, at unpredictable times, comes to haunt and trouble the city commuter, worn and polished like a pebble from routine, while he yawns over his folded newspaper or gazes unseeing out of the steamy window of worker-packed bus or train.

PLATE 35
Calm, cloud and contoured hills and mountains at Glendhu Bay, Lake Wanaka.

A N OCCUPATIONAL HAZARD of deer hunters—those among the 140 professional deer killers paid by the New Zealand Government to curb these "noxious animals" as they are officially classified—is stomach ulcers! Some have to give up finally because of these. It's a man's life; and the hills and the wet, the long hours and the rough tucker, crack back at a man in the end.

Peter Cape ends his song *Black Matai* with:

The stink of the deerskin, the weight of the rifle,
This 80-lb pack that keeps dragging me down.
I'll get out of the mountains and back to the sheepyards.
But my love's left the station, she's gone to the town.

Most of our best shooters are small nuggety men, quick on their feet, smiling, often with strong penetrating blue eyes. Such a man (with brown eyes), Percy Lyes of Hokitika, a professional hunter for eight years, collected 4,000 red deer in that time, roving the bluffs, ravines, and razor-back spurs of the Southern Alps, above the bushline, 4,000 feet up. His best day's total was 69 deer; about a dozen times he's shot over 50 in a day.

His friend Max Curtis of Nelson (where the first deer was liberated in the mid-nineteenth century, to multiply fantastically) got 101 deer in one day at Price Basin, up the Whitcombe River. The two, working together, shot 3,063 deer in one season. In 1955, on the Hunter Dingle Block, the highest in Southland, Wattie Cameron and Frank Woolf shot 2,063 and 2,038 deer respectively.

Poisoned baits, too, are dropped by aircraft in selected areas, and professional meat hunters are also up with the times and on the move by the New Zealand invented jet-boats, up the rivers, and by helicopters into rough, remote mountains, especially if venison is to be packed out for export: about 3 million lbs of venison go overseas a year, mainly to a country of other good shooters, Germany.

PLATE 36
A deer hunter with his packhorses working along a Westland riverbed.

THE GREAT HAAST ROAD, shouldering its way regardless through spectacular bush, mountain, valley, and rampaging river alike, at last links Otago with South Westland, late in 1965 completing a road round the South Island. Travellers rejoice in comfort; lonely outback families have many a burden and anxiety lifted; no longer must remote cattlemen guide and drive their animals on long journeys where the going is rough and tough—and certainly often wet, as well.

A symbol of this achievement is The Bulldozer Which Couldn't Wait for the Road—but pushed on by itself, blazing and hewing its own unique trail, over gruesome going where no vehicle had ever been before, to reach Haast under its own power early in 1954, and joined in work on the still-incomplete road. Three Reefton men, Ray Smith (driver), Eddie Storey (spare driver), and Maurie Hartley took the 23-ton, 130-horsepower yellow bulldozer through the wilderness from road-end at little Paringa to Haast, 38 miles in 38 days, towing behind a wooden sledge loaded with fuel, wire rope, bedding, tools, food—and a dozen beer.

"She'll be right," they said.

The 'dozer's blade in front, 13 feet long and 3 feet high, cleared the smaller trees out of the way; she'd winch herself up steep places; sometimes she crawled along, smothered in a massed canopy of torn vines; mastered 2 miles of black swamp past Lake Moeraki in just over three hours; and in one particular day of triumph, climbed 800 feet up a bush-covered ridge. Then, days of pelting rain, with flooded creeks and rivers cutting them off, food and fuel running out......

But they made it finally, down through giant ratas to Bullock Creek, round past bluffs and creeks, past Ship Creek and Maori River, and finally over the great Haast River itself and to journey's end, on the job.

With men like that—and their companions in construction—the road *had* to go through.

PLATE 37
Hereford cattle crossing the Okuru River, South Westland.

HERE ARE the world's most considerate glaciers, everything but airconditioned and fruit-flavoured, Fox and Franz Josef Glaciers, nearly side by side in the thick bush, named after a New Zealand prime minister and an Austrian emperor.

They come down obligingly to less than 900 feet above sea level, within a couple of miles of the road and your car, hotel, motel, or motor camp. It's hot and warm on Fox and Franz Josef most times, and every year about 5,000 people of all ages go up onto each one, the adventurers including a boy of four-and-a-half, people with artificial limbs, and a veteran of 84—a retired high-country musterer from Canterbury, who beat the lot and raced the glacier guides out of sight coming home. As for the glaciers, they move about 2 feet a day, considered almost shamefully fast in the glacier world.

To fly down the glacier in the small observation plane running regularly for visitors is to ride a fantastic merrygoround, corkscrewing down a river of ice some 9 miles long and almost 1 mile wide. You whirl down the glacier between two tremendous dark walls, and down below you, spinning round and round, are ice pinnacles 150 feet high: a memory you'll never forget.

Fox and Franz Josef grow and flow from the vast snow and icefields packing down high in the Southern Alps. Sir Edmund Hillary, his men, with their huskies and equipment, trained and shook down together high up the Tasman in 1956, before sailing far south to build and occupy New Zealand's Scott Base in that endless extension of our alpine adventures and wonders, the Antarctic.

PLATE 38
Fox Glacier, viewed through a grove of kahikatea trees, Westland.

REMEMBER THE GOLDMINERS.

Here they grovelled and groped for gold in sand, muck, and rubble, between the toes of the indifferent Alps; with rain and sandflies swarming they slaved and panned, sluiced and scraped, and the New Zealand-invented gold dredge came to groan and grind the soil away, to leave vast wormtracks of boulders, a blighted trail, still ruined today, 500 tons of droppings to dredge 1 oz. of gold in the last years of these giant land-locusts.

In the end, most of the miners collected only a living wage and rheumatism. But they left a more enduring mark on the people. Tough and mainly honest adventurers with inquiring minds, they shook the land upside down socially and politically, they questioned and they sluiced for the truth and the "why?" of Life around camp fires and committees. They beat the trackless bush and mountain and rugged coastline, their slogan was "give 'it a go'", and "Jack's as good as his master" and, like the average Kiwi today, they stoutly believed you cannot have liberty and fraternity until you have equality. Seddon stood on their shoulders.

Listen to the echo of their claims: Sunrise, Golden Fleece, South Pole, Nil Desperandum, Corrie's Reward, Wealth of Nations, Keep-it-Dark, Homeward Bound. . . .

Without the goldminers, refrigeration and electricity we might have become a sort of rancid New Caledonia of the South Pacific.

But the miners' streets were mud, the drunkard reeled, the avaricious dug in their claws, and women wept in the eternal rain for yesterdays beyond the wet mountains.

PLATE 39
The Southern Alps, mirrored in quiet waters, Gillespie Beach, Westland.

THIS IS the setting—the only setting—in which the kotuku or white heron chooses to nest, from September to December, in white pines, kowhai and tree-ferns, along one small part of the Waitangiroto River within 10 miles of this lake near the Franz Josef Glacier. Nesting over, kotuku ranges New Zealand again.

In 1941, when most government departments the world over were involved in killing men, Head Office, Lands and Survey Department, hearing sawmillers were approaching these few remote birds, insisted that they were "not to be disturbed in any way".

To give an expert appraisal, Bob Falla (then at the Christchurch Museum), E. V. Stewart (State Forest Service), and Basil King (Commissioner of Crown Lands, Hokitika) paddled up this almost forgotten river, to find only a few odd nests, eight white herons, and six young. No more.

"Unless their breeding-place is protected immediately, they'll soon be extinct," reported Dr Falla, advising the employment of a ranger for the breeding season.

Lands and Survey immediately banned milling during the nesting season. Tom Casey, of nearby Okarito, an ideal choice for a ranger, would need a hut and a boat costing up to NZ$200.00 in all, but public money (the war was costing New Zealand almost NZ$1 million a day then, in 1942) could not be spent unless the birds nested there for sure year by year.

In 1943, Commissioner King found 12 adults and 12 fledgelings: "A crime to let the herons become extinct at this stage," he wrote.

Early 1944, somebody was shooting the shags in the river: the herons next? Head Office, Lands and Survey, promptly paid £50 for a ranger for the four nesting months, and Tom Casey, now ranger, began patrolling the river, sleeping in a tent.

In 1949, 24 adult birds, 19 chicks. By 1959, 54 birds. Today, almost a national symbol, the colony numbers about 50 to 60 white herons. Nesting has levelled out to about 28 nests—they don't nest until four years old. Government file no. 3/181 in Hokitika tells it all. Fifty-five miles south the kotuku nests safely in this setting today—but it was a close thing.

NOT ON THIS august road, of course, but further inland, on a more modest route, an inspecting engineer went butcher's hook at the old West Coast roadman. "What a travesty of a road," thundered the visitor: "badly drained, atrocious surface, blind corners, a wretched grade, far too steep, much too narrow."

The old roadman heard him out in silence, to the very end, when he looked the official dead in the eye and asked patiently: "Yeah. And how's she *for length?*"

Another heroic West Coast roadman is venerated by Archdeacon James Young, vicar of Ross and South Westland 1923–28, riding his parish mostly on horseback (5,700 miles a year, old Bessie wearing out a set of horse shoes every four weeks). This remote roadman, in his fifties, was painfully struggling to teach himself to read from (of all things) a volume of Hansard!

"A man with a great heart, by jove," said the archdeacon, who mercifully came to the student's rescue within a fortnight with an urgent bundle of Education Department readers.

In an even more remote spot, further south yet, this backblocks clergyman soon grew to admire a roadman keeping the packtracks clear. He'd lived alone for some 10 years in a tiny, exceedingly dark hut, with no window. The archdeacon and a friend packed in, in secret, over bluff, spur and riverbed, a glass window. Then, seeing the roadman wasn't in, they cut a hole by the chimney and installed the window, as a surprise.

Just before sunset, the roadman returned, to the new window glinting golden. He walked around his hut like a man in a trance, as if it were the Crystal Palace, speechless with admiration. Then he went inside—but soon emerged, troubled and frowning, from his transformed hut.

"God save us!" exclaimed the roadman. "Isn't it *dirty* in there!"

PLATE 41
Meybelle Bay, looking north along the Westport-Greymouth section of Highway 6.

THE ROUGH, tough, touslehaired, stringy, scrawny, she'll-be-right, unkillable, likable cabbage-tree—old-timers used to weave shady hats from its long leaves—can predict the weather by its abundance—or not—of early white bundles of flowers; but when the summer does come, nobody can remember if it flowered well or not, and which or what indicates, anyhow, a wet or dry summer?

Rata sets the West Coast ablaze at Christmas and New Year, some rata—on the true-traveller's road through the clouds and the clematis to Karamea—looking like towers of dark blood, an astonishing sight with memory stitching a fine thread of fear through it later. A much gentler hunter of travellers' thoughts is the clematis, flinging so carelessly and so correctly a wild net of springtime stars.

The people around here?
"They're an honest lot," said the baker, Mr Bishop of Granity, who supplied them with bread for years. "When I sold my business I'd no fear of bad debts. Every solitary single one of them paid up—as I knew they would."

Yet all is not gleam and goodwill. Some rivers were named the Widow-Makers. The lakes with dark waters give wonderful reflections, yet a beauty only skin-deep perhaps, and really rather sinister. If you shoot a wild duck, you'll have to row for your life to pick it up, for in an instant the gay feathers will begin a sudden weird bobbing and dancing on the water, and if you aren't quick the giant eels will pull it down, ending the ballet.

PLATE 42
A roadside cabbage tree on the coastline north of Punakaiki.

"LARGE GRANITE ROCKS heaped confusedly together all over the surface, with a thick growth of underbrush and briers, an immense quantity of dead and rotten timber, and all these on the steep and broken declivities of a range of high mountain, interspersed with perpendicular walls of rocks, precipices and deep ravines, form a combination of difficulties which must be encountered to be adequately understood or allowed for." (Thomas Brunner.)

Brunner explored the Buller (accompanied by two Maoris *and their wives*) in the first half of 1847. His report is a classic of survival and arrowhead determination scarcely even hinted at in this modest quotation.

Next to New Zealand's largest river (the Clutha) in volume pouring into the sea, this turbulent, powerful Buller, in places looking like an immense smooth grey-green serpent moving imperturbably and imperiously on its way, is named not after a truly heroic explorer like Brunner who, clothing reduced to rags and tatters, really sweated and fought it out even to the extent of eating fungus, fernroots and the dog Rover, to survive and to trap and pin the great river's secret twistings and carvings on the map. Instead, it takes its name from an English member of Parliament whose "conduct in the New Zealand debates (in the British Parliament) connected his name with the history of the Colony."

But what *could* he have said to deserve such a river?

PLATE 43
The Buller River, west of Berlins, on the Inangahua Junction/Westport Highway.

"THERE IS a fresh water mussel abounding in the Rotoroa, called the kaiehau, which, boiled with the roots of the raupo, or bulrush, makes a palatable dish, and was the favourite meal of the celebrated savage Rauparaha." (Thomas Brunner, making the best of Christmas Eve, 1846, at the neighbouring lake.)

Indeed, the way of the explorer and the surveyor, these unsung heroes of New Zealand, was hard.

Close to this lake, Rotoiti, swung one of New Zealand's most historic sheep trails, the old Rainbow Track, noisy with great mobs to stock the new runs of Canterbury and even of Otago. This track, once known as the Main South Road, and even considered for a time as suitable for a Christchurch-Nelson railway, is tramped today by a line of silent silver giants, pylons carrying the powerlines of the South Island's main grid.

The old trail heads south, doggedly down the mountainous middle of the South Island, twisting up to over 4,000 feet, far from the distant coast and flat lands, following along in turn the headwaters of the Wairau and Clarence Rivers, to emerge at Hanmer, where the sheep were sent on to Culverden, which was linked by rail with Christchurch on a great day in February 1886.

More than half of Canterbury's imported sheep in 1864 had been driven overland from Nelson—38,050 of them, records a Nelson historian, J. N. W. Newport, in *Footprints*. The trip took about three weeks, at the sensible pace of 10 miles journeying a day, in the season between January and April. Some mobs, at the modest charge of 20c. a head, ranged from 4,000 to 6,000 sheep, needing in some parts up to 15 drovers. Two men could comfortably handle mobs of 1,000 to 1,500 sheep.

But since the middle 'twenties, few mobs have passed along the old Rainbow Track in the shadows of the Spenser Mountains.

PLATE 44
Lake Rotoiti, Nelson, under clear blue skies and spring sunshine.

SOME OF THE clay hillsides now covered in plump orchards were once considered completely useless for anything, and were joyfully sold off if an extraordinary offer came for less than a dollar an acre. ("Those were the good old days, when half a dollar was half a dollar, *but we didn't have half a dollar,*" as Alan Brown, applefarmer, puts it.)

Orchards, lovely to look at and heavy with fruit, fill mountains of cases every season as the sweating orchardists and workers know only too well: 2,300,000 cases of apples and pears from Nelson with about 1,800,000 of them exported overseas: Gravensteins, Cox's Orange, Cleopatras, Jonathan, William's Bon Chretien (a pear, that one), Delicious, Sturmer, Granny Smiths, Doughertys...picking from January to about May. The "help yourself" honesty stalls of fruits and vegetables restore faith to the dry and the doubting.

"Only God can make a tree. Very well," runs another typical orchardist remark, "but you could add another verse to that song. Only an orchardist can keep it in good shape *commercially* over the years if it's a blessed fruit tree."

But well before all this, the pride and joy of the Maoris of Appleby pa was their elaborately carved canoe, Te Awatea, a thing of beauty, speed and grace. Rampaging North Islanders seized this great canoe and made off with it to their stronghold, Kapiti Island, on the other side of Cook Strait. In time of national gloom or peril, this canoe is said to appear again, crowded with chanting warriors paddling the old war-trail.

But for all the uproar it hasn't been sighted this century— too violent, even for a cannibal canoe?

PLATE 45
Orchards at Appleby near Richmond in the fruitgrowing province of Nelson.

FROM KAITERITERI to Farewell Spit lies a remarkable strand of beaches, many of them literally golden-orange in colour, most of them making Honolulu's fabled beach look like an old hen's dustbath. The beauty of this safe and sunny coast, with its bush and mountain and 45,000-acre National Park, will some day be enjoyed to the full by holidaymakers, as Picton is today.

Somewhere close to Ligar Bay the Dutch explorer Abel Janszoon Tasman, seeking fresh water, wood, and refreshments, anchored his flagship *Heemskerck*, 60 tons, and *Zeehaen*, 100 tons, a week before Christmas in 1642. The Maoris and the Dutch exchanged trumpet blasts, but without goodwill. Next morning, 19 December, four Dutchmen were slain, clubbed to death in their rowing-boat; naming the place with justification "Murderers Bay", Tasman sailed away, landing nowhere in New Zealand.

Nearly two centuries later, in 1827, the famous French explorer and gentleman Jules S. C. D. d'Urville arrived and survived intact to make excellent charts and to name Adèle Island (and an Antarctic penguin) after his wife.

He, like today's travellers, was particularly taken with the friendly little fantails: "extraordinarily bold . . . they carry their confidence so far as to come and perch on your stick or on the barrel of your gun."

PLATE 46
Tata and Ligar beaches, looking west to Takaka district and the distant Tasman Mountains.

AROUND THE CORNER to the left, hurrah for the Golden Bay Cement Works, Nelson's industrial dusty mammoth, established half a century, with its long jetty, its two cement ships *Golden Bay* and *Ligar Bay* hustling in and out, each flat-out ferrying thousands of tons of nation-building, earth-isolating, powdery cement in its own sealed holds to massive silos in Wellington—and to national projects such as X, Y, and Z. Annual output: several pyramids of cement—and much more in the years to come, they predict, just you wait and see. Maybe New Zealand will be *all* concrete one day, entirely covered? Mount Cook too. Onward!

Giants live in the limestone cliffs and caves, perhaps politely tattooed, and invisible to anyone over 10. Robin Hood and feathered Indian, William the Conqueror and Superman, leap and vanish from tall shadowy crevices behind tree-trunks and cliff-vines where the woodpigeon in white overalls gobbles golden or red berries, and maybe a Maori warrior's bone lies cracked, sucked, and lonely.

Girls in loving frocks, never before so beautiful, emerge inscrutable from the fennel, remembering forever the aniseed smell and the sunbeams.

Around the corner to the right the Pohara Motor Camp canteen, green and white as an all-day sucker, run by Edward Jacobsen, who never stops selling things in season, day, night, and moonrise.

Sometimes, alas, the terrible transistor brays out from the otherwise admirable motor camp alongside.

Best of all, by far and away, *peacocks*—bird of the sun and of all Indias—swooping from Peacock Rock on the hill, or from Mrs Manson's roof to the top of the canteen.

About 26 birds, posing for the tourists, shrieking at the cash register, challenging the chromium cars, picking sealice from the Pohara Beach with the grace of gods.... As you were: untrue. They're all gone now—stolen by chuffs?—except one; two were crushed by the cars which brought the people to see the peacocks....

And the sound of the cicadas surges like an electronic storm in summer, and the heat beats down, brown, all brown. Old men slowly circle, stiffly consider, then cautiously sit in dry sand safely above tidemark and katipo, and tell how they fled from Thermopylae, while small children, scuttering like hermit crabs, pry from pool to pool, and find a universe unfolding in a sea anemone.

PLATE 47
Coastline at Tarakohe, looking towards Pohara Beach.

THE RIVERS and the creeks aren't muddy and churned up any more, and you have to search the valleys and hills to find fading scars where once the hungry ones hunted....

"When I first saw Collingwood in February, 1857, there were only two tents in it....In 1858 I again went to Collingwood and there were then seven hotels in it," notes H. P. Washbourn in his *Reminiscences of Early Days*. This indefatigable Nelsonian, a great tramper, inquirer, and observer, thought a gold-rush was rather like "a large camping picnic with everyone in the highest spirits as if they had just come into a fortune or were just about to do so".

New Zealand's first strikes with moderate rushes were at Coromandel and Collingwood. For a while in 1857–58 miners around Collingwood numbered nearly 2,000, but a year later most had faded away. The wife of a butcher-cum-banker sewed deposits of gold into her skirt and made a few trips into Nelson before ships began calling regularly at booming Collingwood—little ships "named *Elizabeth*, *Nancy*, *Rapid*, *Atlanta*, *Mary Thomson*, *Necromancer*, and *The Sisters*, which sank at Totaranui through a stupid bullock putting his foot through the bottom of her". Bullocks, sometimes worked to death, packed in loads of about 3 cwt each over punishing country to the miners. There were no roads.

The Perseverance mine, detected in Bedstead Gully (Mr McGregor, a disappointed prospector, had left his camp bed there in chagrin) near Collingwood in 1866, was one of the South Island's first quartz mines, yielding gold from crushing for a number of years.

The first year of the Collingwood rush gave 10,437 oz.— today, the district produces golden butter—700 tons of it a year.

PLATE 48
Tidal waters at Collingwood, Nelson Province.

IN THIS RIVER, in 1843, five years before the discovery of gold in California, a surveyor's chainman, James Spittal, found a piece of our earliest gold, the size of a French bean; but land was the great hunger then. Not until 1857 were more than a thousand miners hard at it around the Aorere.

The Heaphy Track, beginning here, deserves to be much better known, and publicised, preserved and used. It begins 9 miles from Bainham post office, is 40 miles long, and takes three to four days to traverse. The scenery and birdlife (including kiwis) are well worth while: heavy bush country to the highest point, 3,000 feet; the Gouland Downs (deer, pig, duck); fine birch forest and bold river; five hours along the coast with featherduster nikau palms and flax and stinging-nettle, to the Kohaihai Bluff and River; then it's 10 miles to Karamea the Blest—gay lights, hotel, and aerodrome.

The Heaphy Track, the old gold-diggers' trail, could become a Milford Track of the north.

The veteran tramper A.H. Reed made the Heaphy a few days after his eighty-ninth birthday, and "can thoroughly recommend it—but not for those just entering their ninetieth year".

PLATE 49
The Aorere River, south of Bainham, at the northern end of the Heaphy Track.

THERE IS a green hill far away.....

Standing here you are well north of Wellington without having crossed Cook Strait.

This is the bow of the Great Canoe where Maui hauled up the poor fish of the North Island.

A place of few settlements, no crowds, and long, lovely, lonely beaches like Pakawau; a place of inlets and sun-beams, of bird-tracks along tidal estuaries, and a little pocket-Marlborough Sounds, unknown and unheeded, fringed with bush, tall nikau palms, and curious hanging greenery. Sometimes, a spot black with swans.

Close, now, to the top of the South Island, like the head of a green kiwi, with Farewell Spit its tawny beak.

Among the last of these green hills lives farmer Jack Richards, 86. Alone for 55 years, up wild seacoast and across mudflats to reach a road, he used to drive his own remote cattle 120 miles to Nelson.

Along this way, 100 years ago, late one cold frosty June night in the 'sixties, came H. P. Washbourn and his brother. Rather than freeze, they entered one of New Zealand's earliest hotels, "a large Maori whare with a chimmey at one end and a door at the other with a bare ground floor entirely covered with Maoris and Pakehas as thick as they could pack in." The only fare: small potatoes, "1s. 6d. if they cooked them, and 9d. if you cooked them yourself." The only drink: a so-called "rum". Bedding: no blankets, not even a layer of cut fern or manuka; just the bare earth floor.

PLATE 50
Sunlight and shadows enhance along a country roadway in the Kaihoka district.

BLUE HILLS, blue shadows caressing Crusader's brave profile as all wars over forever he sleeps his skyline sleep under the big blue sky, blue Tasman Bay, blue Golden Bay, blue colours on the football jerseys, blue flag flying with its three-book crest over Nelson College, blue fingers in piping crisp frosty winters....

Great golden chrysanthemums airfreighted around New Zealand, golden beaches, golden Golden Bay, golden fruit, flakes and colours of gold still to be panned in many a stream, golden daffodils in century-old clumps, the golden Maitai River of the autumn College boys and girls, golden wattle, the golden-coloured football jerseys, golden marigolds burning by batches, golden broom, golden gorse...

The surveyors, and later the settlers, sailed into blue-and-gold when they made landfall here: the first of all ships the brig *Arrow* carrying stores in November 1841; and later the first immigrant ship *Fifeshire* (16 deaths on the voyage), in February 1842. *Fifeshire* herself died at the end of that month with a broken back by the great rock with two names to the left of this scene—Arrow Rock or Fifeshire Rock (take your choice) to mark these two pioneer ships.

Unhappily, no longer slipping through the cut in the Boulder Bank comes the Nelson ferryboat, reeking and reeling from Cook Strait buffetings, or in an unbelievable calm and stillness which made early morning passengers gaze in wonder, and whisper.

The Nelson railway (the only provincial capital without a railway) is ripped up, and politicians' promises rust and rot in the Buller Gorge, and elsewhere. Over the years of expectation, copper, iron, building marble, and asbestos works have closed down—even uranium developments came to a halt.

New life may lie within man-made forests, timber and paper, intensive market gardening, and new demands for the wide variety of minerals, in a place of great beauty and almost perfect climate.

Farewell to the first of the South, the Cinderella province, blue and gold.....

THANKS

First and foremost to the incomparable *Making New Zealand*, pictorial surveys of a century, issued by the New Zealand Government 1939–40 to mark our first 100 years of organised European settlement. *Making New Zealand* brought our own history alive, for the first time, made it something to feel and to work from, not to shrug away in impatience and boredom.

Next, "Open Country" friends from Auckland to Invercargill who helped fill in a number of ruts and potholes: Susi R. Collins, Peggy Dunstan, Maurice Flahive, Jeff Newport, Adrian Hayter, Archdeacon James Young, the Washbourn family for nagging their grandfather into writing down his memories, Gerald Goulter, Norman Brayshaw, Bryan Trolove, Reg and Roey Winn, Hilary Heddlestone, Lilliam Rouse, Alister Mackintosh, Tosti Murray, and Fred Miller.

Then *The New Zealand Guide* by Ted Dollimore, a comfort in times of weary blankness; *Nelson* by Ruth M. Allan; the Caxton Press for part of the poem by Mary Ursula Bethell, and the Broadcasting people for assignments over the years to go and see for myself.

Government Departments that I am particularly grateful to, supplying facts promptly and generously, are: Lands and Survey; New Zealand Forest Service; the Grasslands Division and the Crop Research Division of the DSIR; Electricity, Railways, and Marine.

The caption on Tarakohe is dedicated to Hamish Henderson, born and died on 16 March 1966.